THE

NEW-ENGLAND

PRIMER

IMPROVED

For the more easy attaining the true
reading of English.

TO WHICH IS ADDED

The Assembly of Divines, and
Mr. COTTON's *Catechism.*

BOSTON:

Printed by EDWARD DRAPER, *at*
his Printing-Office, in *Newbury-*
Street, and *Sold* by JOHN BOYLE
in *Marlborough-Street.* 1777.

Additional materials available from:
WallBuilders
P. O. Box 397
Aledo, TX 76008
(817) 441-6044
For orders or to obtain a catalog:
Call (800) 873-2845 or visit
www.wallbuilders.com

ISBN 10: 0-925279-17-X

ISBN 13: 978-0-925279-17-0

Foreword

The contents of this edition, with the exception of this foreword, are a camera reproduction of the 1777 *New England Primer* (pronounced "prem' -ur").

The New England Primer, introduced in Boston in 1690 by Benjamin Harris, was the first textbook printed in America. For a century after its introduction, it was **the** beginning textbook for students; and until well into the twentieth century (there was a 1930 edition) it continued to be a principal text in all types of American schools: public, private, semiprivate, home, dame, parochial, etc. The Founders, as well as millions of other Americans, learned to read from *The New England Primer* and the Bible.

Although later editions offered more reading and vocabulary words than the first edition, the *Primer* underwent few significant changes over its 240 years of widespread use. The core of the *Primer* – its rhyming alphabet, alphabet of lessons for youth, Bible questions, and Shorter Catechism – remained largely intact from reprint to reprint.

The value of the Shorter Catechism, an inseparable part of the *Primer*, was explained in the 1843 edition:

> Our Puritan Fathers brought the Shorter Catechism with them across the ocean and laid it on the same shelf with the family Bible. They taught it diligently to their children ... If in this Catechism the true and fundamental doctrines of the Gospel are expressed in fewer and better words and definitions than in any other summary, why ought we not now to train up a child in the way he should go? – why not now put him in possession of the

richest treasure that ever human wisdom and industry accumulated to draw from?

The 1900 edition described the impact of the *Primer*:

> *The New England Primer* was one of the greatest books ever published. It went through innumerable editions; it reflected in a marvelous way the spirit of the age that produced it, and contributed, perhaps more than any other book except the Bible, to the molding of those sturdy generations that gave to America its liberty and its institutions.

May this 2007 reprint of *The New England Primer* once again challenge, inspire, and help mold a sturdy generation of Americans who will significantly contribute to the preservation of America's liberties and institutions!

Helpful Notes to the Reader

- The illustrations in *The New England Primer* reflect the printing of the era in which they were first introduced and used. That is, the illustrations are crude woodcuts and the typeset is small and irregular; both were typical features of the hand-engraving, hand-typesetting, and hand-printing on the slow hand-operated machines of that era.

- In the *Primer*, our letter "s" often appears as "f" or "ſ," and an "ss" appears as "ff" or "ſſ." To our eyes, this initially creates visual confusion. However, the eye and brain tend to rapidly adjust and compensate, particularly with younger students. Soon, these unusual substitutes for our familiar "s" become no hindrance in reading and understanding the *Primer*.

- *The New England Primer* was a text for students who were just beginning to read, regardless of their age (there were no grade level classifications in American schools until the 19th century). While the *Primer* is therefore the equivalent of a first-grade textbook, it probably is well above the reading and vocabulary level of today's typical first-graders – a potent commentary on the difference between the educational systems of then and now!

David Barton
May 2007

THE

NEW-ENGLAND

PRIMER

IMPROVED

For the more easy attaining the true

reading of English.

TO WHICH IS ADDED

The Assembly of Divines, and

Mr. COTTON's *Catechism.*

BOSTON:

Printed by EDWARD DRAPER, *at*
his Printing-Office, in *Newbury-*
Street, and *Sold* by JOHN BOYLE
in *Marlborough-Street.*　1777.

The Honorable JOHN HANCOCK, Efq:
Prefident of the *American* CONGRESS

A Divine Song of Praife to G O D, for a Child,
by the Rev. Dr. WATTS.

*HOW glorious is our heavenly King,
Who reigns above the Sky!
How shall a Child presume to sing
His dreadful Majesty!*

*How great his Power is none can tell,
Nor think how large his Grace:
Nor men below, nor Saints that dwell
On high before his Face.*

*Nor Angels that stand round the Lord,
Can search his secret will;
But they perform his heav'nly Word,
And sing his Praises still.*

*Then let me join this holy Train;
And my first Off'rings bring;
The eternal GOD will not disdain
To hear an Infant sing.*

*My Heart resolves, my Tongue obeys,
And Angels shall rejoice,
To hear their mighty Maker's Praise,
Sound from a feeble Voice.*

The young INFANT'S or CHILD'S morning Prayer. *From Dr.* WATTS.

ALMIGHTY God the Maker of every Thing in Heaven and Earth; the Darkneſs goes away, and the Day light comes at thy Command. Thou art good and doeſt good continually.

I thank thee that thou haſt taken ſuch Care of me this Night, and that I am alive and well this Morning.

Save me, O God, from Evil, all this Day long, and let me love and ſerve thee forever, for the Sake of Jeſus Chriſt thy Son. AMEN.

The INFANT'S or young CHILD'S Evening Prayer. *From* Dr. WATTS.

O LORD God who knoweſt all Things, thou ſeeſt me by Night as well as by Day.

I pray thee for Chriſt's Sake, forgive me whatſoever I have done amiſs this Day, and keep me all this Night, while I am aſleep.

I deſire to lie down under thy Care, and to abide forever under thy Bleſſing, for thou art a God of all Power and everlaſting Mercy. AMEN.

a b c d e f g h i j k l m

n o p q r ſ s t u v

w x y z &.

Vowels.

a e i o u y.

Conſonants.

b c d ſ g h j k l m n p q r ſ s t v w x z

Double Letters.

ct ff fi fl ffi ffl ſh ſi ſſi ſl ff ſt

Italick Letters.

Aa Bb Cc Dd Ee Ff Gg Hh
Ii Jj Kk Ll Mm Nn Oo Pp Qq
Rr Sſs Tt Uu Vv Ww Xx Yy Zz

Italick Double Letters.

ct ff fi ffi fl ffl ſh ſi ſſ ſſi ſl ſt.

Great Letters.

A B C D E F G H I J K L M N O

P Q R S T U W X Y Z.

Ab	eb	ib	ob	ub
ac	ec	ic	oc	uc
ad	ed	id	od	ud
af	ef	if	of	uf
ag	eg	ig	og	ug
aj	ej	ij	oj	uj
ak	ek	ik	ok	uk
al	el	il	ol	ul
am	em	im	om	um
an	en	in	on	un
ap	ep	ip	op	up
ar	er	ir	or	ur
as	es	is	os	us
at	et	it	ot	ut
av	ev	iv	ov	uv
ax	ex	ix	ox	ux
az	ez	iz	oz	uz

Eaſy

Eafy Syllables, &c.

Ba	be	bi	bo	bu
ca	ce	ci	co	cu
da	de	di	do	da
fa	fe	fi	fo	fu
ga	ge	gi	go	gu
ha	he	hi	ho	hu
ja	je	ji	jo	ju
ka	ke	ki	ko	ku
la	le	li	lo	lu
ma	me	mi	mo	mu
na	ne	ni	no	nu
pa	pe	pi	po	pu
ra	re	ri	ro	ru
ſa	ſe	ſi	ſo	fu
ta	te	ti	to	tu
va	ve	vi	vo	vu
wa	we	wi	wo	wu
ya	ye	yi	yo	yu
za	ze	zi	zo	zu

Words of one Syllable.

Age	all	ape	are
Babe	beef	beſt	bold
Cat	cake	crown	cup
Deaf	dead	dry	dull

Words of one Syllable.

Eat	ear	eggs	eyes
Face	feet	fiſh	foul
Gate	good	graſs	great
Hand	hat	head	heart
Ice	ink	iſle	jobb
Kick	kind	kneel	know
Lamb	lame	land	long
Made	mole	moon	mouth
Name	night	noiſe	noon
Oak	once	one	ounce
Pain	pair	pence	pound
Quart	queen	quick	quilt
Rain	raiſe	roſe	run
Saint	ſage	ſalt	ſaid
Take	talk	time	throat
Vain	vice	vile	view
Way	wait	waſte	would

Words of two Syllables.

Ab-ſent	ab-hor	a-pron	au-thor
Ba-bel	be-came	be-guile	bold-ly
Ca-pon	cel-lar	con-ſtant	cub-board
Dai-ly	de-pend	di-vers	du-ty
Ea-gle	ea-ger	en-close	e-ven
Fa-ther	fa-mous	fe-male	fu-ture
Ga-ther	gar-den	gra-vy	glo-ry

Words of two Syllables.

Hei-nous	hate-ful	hu-mane	hus-band
In-fant	in-deed	in-cence	i-ſland
Ja-cob	jeal-ous	juſ-tice	ju-lep
La-bour	la-den	la-dy	la-zy
Ma-ny	ma-ry	mo-tive	mu-ſick

Words of three Syllables.

A-bu-ſing	a-mend-ing	ar-gu-ment
Bar-ba-rous	be-ne-fit	beg-gar-ly
Cal-cu-late	can-dle-stick	con-ſoun-ded
Dam-ni-fy	dif-fi-cult	drow-ſi-neſs
Ea-ger-ly	em-ploy-ing	evi-dence
Fa-cul-ty	fa-mi-ly	fu-ne-ral
Gar-de-ner	glo-ri-ous	gra-ti-tude
Hap-pi-ness	har-mo-ny	ho-li-neſs

Words of four Syllables.

A-bi-li-ty	ac-com-pa-ny	af-fec-ti-on
Be-ne-fi-ted	be-a-ti-tude	be-ne-vo-lent
Ca-la-mi-ty	ca-pa-ci-ty	ce-re-mo-ny
De-li-ca-cy	di-li-gent-ly	du-ti-ful-ly
E-dy-ſy-ing	e-ver-laſt-ing	e-vi-dent-ly
Fe-bru-a-ry	fi-de-li-ty	for-mi-da-bly
Ge-ne-ral-ly	glo-ri-ſy-ing	gra-ci-ous-ly

Words of five Syllables.

A-bo-mi-na-ble	ad-mi-ra-ti-on
Be-ne-dic-ti-on	be-ne-fi-ci-al
Ce-le-bra-ti-on	con-fo-la-ti-on
De-cla-ra-ti-on	de-di-ca-ti-on
E-du-ca-ti-on	ex-hor-ta-ti-on
For-ni-ca-ti-on	fer-men-ta-ti-on
Ge-ne-ra-ti-on	ge-ne-ro-fi-ty

Words of fix Syllables.

A-bo-mi-na-ti-on	Gra-ti-fi-ca-ti-on
Be-ne-fi-ci-al-ly	Hu-mi-li-a-ti-on
Con-ti-nu-a-ti-on	I-ma-gi-na-ti-on
De-ter-mi-na-ti-on	Mor-ti-fi-ca-ti-on
E-di-fi-ca-ti-on	Pu-ri-fi-ca-ti-on
Fa-mi-li-a-ri-ty	Qua-li-fi-ca-ti-on

A Lesson for Children.

Pray to God.	Call no ill names.
Love God.	Ufe no ill words.
Fear God.	Tell no lies.
Serve God.	Hate Lies.
Take not God's Name in vain.	Speak the Truth. Spend your Time well.
Do not Swear.	Love your School.
Do not Steal.	Mind your Book.
Cheat not in your play.	Strive to learn.
Play not with bad boys.	Be not a Dunce.

A   In ADAM's Fall
We finned all.

B   Heaven to find,
The Bible Mind.

C   Chrift crucify'd
For finners dy'd.

D   The Deluge drown'd
The Earth around.

E   ELIJAH hid
By Ravens fed.

F   The judgment made
FELIX afraid.

G As runs the Glass,
   Our Life doth pass.

H My Book and Heart
   Must never part.

I JOB feels the Rod,—
   Yet bleſſes GOD.

K Proud Korah's troop
   Was ſwallowed up

L LOT fled to *Zoar*,
   Saw fiery Shower
   On *Sodom* pour.

M MOSES was he
   Who *Israel's* Hoſt
   Led thro' the Sea

N O A H did view
The old world & new.

O Young O B A D I A S,
D A V I D, J O S I A S,
All were pious.

P P E T E R deny'd
His Lord and cry'd.

Q Queen E S T H E R ſues
And ſaves the *Jews.*

R Young pious R U T H,
Left all for Truth.

S Young S A M ' L dear,
The Lord did fear.

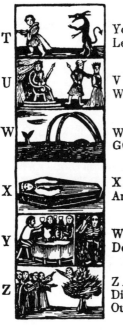

T — Young T I M O T H Y
Learnt fin to fly.

U — V A S T H I for Pride,
Was fet afide.

W — Whales in the Sea,
GOD's Voice obey.

X — X E R X E S did die,
And fo muft I.

Y — While youth do chear
Death may be near.

Z — Z A C C H E U S he
Did climb the Tree
Our Lord to fee.

WHO was the firſt man ? *Adam.*
Who was the firſt woman ? *Eve.*
Who was the firſt Murderer ? *Cain.*
Who was the firſt Martyr ? *Abel.*
Who was the firſt Tranſlated ? *Enoch.*
Who was the oldeſt Man ? *Methuſelah.*
Who built the Ark ? *Noah.*
Who was the Patienteſt Man ? *Job.*
Who was the Meekeſt Man ? *Moſes.*
Who led *Iſrael* into *Canaan* ? *Joſhua.*
Who was the ſtrongeſt Man ? *Sampſon.*
Who killed *Goliah* ? *David.*
Who was the wiſeſt Man ? *Solomon.*
Who was in the Whale's Belly ? *Jonah.*
Who ſaves loſt Men ? *Jeſus Chriſt.*
Who is *Jeſus Chriſt* ? *The Son of God.*
Who was the Mother of *Chriſt* ? *Mary.*
Who betrayed his Maſter ? *Judas.*
Who denied his Maſter ? *Peter.*
Who was the firſt Chriſtian Martyr ? *Stephen.*
Who was chief Apoſtle of the *Gentiles* ? *Paul.*

The Infant's Grace before and after Meat.

BLESS me, O Lord, and let my food ſtrengthen me to ſerve thee, for Jeſus Chriſt's ſake. AMEN.

I Deſire to thank God who gives me food to eat every day of my life. AMEN.

WHAT's right and good now ſhew me Lord, and lead me by thy grace and word. Thus ſhall I be a child of God, and love and fear thy hand and rod.

An Alphabet of Leſſons for Youth.

A Wiſe ſon maketh a glad father, but a fooliſh ſon is the heavineſs of his mother.

BEtter is a little with the fear of the Lord, than great treaſure & trouble therewith.

COme unto Chriſt all ye that labor and are heavy laden and he will give you reſt.

DO not the abominable thing which I hate faith the Lord.

EXcept a man be born again, he cannot ſee the kingdom of God.

FOoliſhneſs is bound up in the heart of a child, but the rod of correction ſhall drive it far from him.

GODLINESS is profitable unto all things, having the promiſe of the life that now is, and that which is to come.

HOLINESS becomes G O D ' s houſe for ever.

IT is good for me to draw near unto G O D.

KEEP thy heart with all diligence, **for** out of it are the issues of life.

LIARS shall have their part in the lake which burns with fire and brimstone.

MANY are the afflictions of the righteous, but the Lord delivereth them out of them all.

NOW is the accepted time, now is **the** day of salvation.

OUT of the abundance of the heart the mouth speaketh.

PRAY to thy Father which is in secret; and thy Father which sees in secret shall reward thee openly.

QUIT you like men, be strong, stand **fast** in the faith.

REMEMBER thy Creator **in the days** of thy youth.

SEest thou a man wise in his own **conceit**, there is more hope of a fool than of him.

TRUST in God at all times, ye people, pour out your hearts before him.

UPON the wicked, God shall rain **an** horrible tempest.

WO to the wicked, it shall be ill with him, for the reward of his **hands** shall be given him.

E**X**HORT one another daily while it is called to day, left any of you be hardened thro' the deceitfulnefs of fin.

YOUNG men ye have overcome the wicked one.

ZEal hath confumed me, becaufe thy enemies have forgotten the word of God.

The LORD's Prayer.

OUR Father which art in heaven, hallowed be thy name. Thy kingdom come. Thy will be done on earth as it is heaven. Give us this day our daily bread. And forgive us our debts as we forgive our debtors. And lead us not into temptation. But deliver us from evil. For thine is the kingdom, the power and the glory, forever. A M E N.

The C R E E D.

I BELIEVE in God the Father Almighty Maker of heaven and earth, and in Jefus Chrift his only Son our Lord, which was conceived by the Holy Ghoft, born of the Virgin Mary, fuffered under Pontius Pilate, was crucified, dead and buried. He defcended into hell. The third day he arofe again from the dead, and afcended into heaven, and fitteth on the right hand of God, the Father,

Almighty. From thence he ſhall come to judge both the quick and the dead. I believe in the Holy Ghoſt, the Holy Catholic Church, the communion of Saints, the forgiveneſs of ſins, the reſurrection of the body, and the life everlaſting. AMEN.

Dr. WATTS's *Cradle Hymn.*

HUSH my dear, lie ſtill and ſlumber,
   holy angels guard thy bed,
Heavenly bleſſings without number,
   gently falling on thy head.
Sleep my babe, thy food and raiment
   houſe and home thy friends provide,
All without thy care or payment,
   all thy wants are well ſupply'd.
How much better thou'rt attended,
   than the Son of God could be,
When from heaven he deſcended,
   and became a child like thee.
Soft and eaſy is thy cradle,
   coarſe and hard thy Saviour lay,
When his birth-place was a ſtable,
   and his ſofteſt bed was hay.
Bleſſed Babe ! what glorious features
   ſpotleſs fair, divinely bright ! !
Muſt he dwell with brutal creatures,

how could angels bear the fight!
Was there nothing but a manger,
   curfed finners could afford,
To receive the heavenly ftranger;
   did they thus affront their Lord.
Soft my child I did not chide thee,
   tho' my fong may found too hard;
'Tis thy mother fits befide thee,
   and her arms fhall be thy guard.
Yet to read the fhameful ftory,
   how the Jews abus'd their King,
How they ferv'd the Lord of glory,
   makes me angry while I fing.
See the kinder fhepherds round him,
   telling wonders from the fky;
There they fought him, there they found him,
   with his Virgin Mother by.
See the lovely Babe a dreffing;
   lovely Infant how he smil'd!
When he wept, the Mother's bleffing
   sooth'd and hufh'd the holy child.
Lo! he flumbers in his manger,
   where the horned oxen fed;
Peace my darling here's no danger
   here's no Ox a near thy bed.
'Twas to fave thee, child from dying,
   fave my dear from burning flame,

Bitter groans and endlefs crying,
    that thy bleft Redeemer came.
May'ft thou live to know and fear him,
    truft and love him all thy days!
Then go dwell for ever near him,
    fee his face and fing his praife.
I could give thee thoufand kiffes,
    hoping what I moft defire:
Not a mother's fondeft wifhes,
    can to greater joys afpire.

VERSES *for Children.*

THOUGH I am young a little one,
    If I can fpeak and go alone,
Then I muft learn to know the Lord,
And learn to read his holy word.
'Tis time to feek to God and pray
For what I want for every day:
I have a precious foul to fave,
And I a mortal body have,
Tho' I am young yet I may die,
And haften to eternity:
There is a dreadful fiery hell,
Where wicked ones must always dwell:
There is a heaven full of joy,
Where godly ones must always ftay:
To one of thefe my foul must fly,
    As in a moment when I die:

When God that made me, calls me home,
I muſt not ſtay I muſt be gone.
He gave me life, and gives me breath,
And he can ſave my ſoul from death,
By JESUS CHRIST my only Lord,
According to his holy word.
He clothes my back and makes me warm:
He ſaves my fleſh and bones from harm.
He gives me bread and milk and meat
And all I have that's good to eat.
When I am ſick, he if he pleaſe,
Can make me well and give me eaſe:
He gives me ſleep and quiet reſt,
Whereby my body is refreſh'd
The Lord is good and kind to me,
And very thankful I muſt be:
I muſt obey and love and fear him,
By faith in Chriſt I muſt draw near him.
I muſt not ſin as others do,
Leſt I lie down in ſorrow too:
For God is angry every day,
With wicked ones who go aſtray,
All ſinful words I muſt reſtrain:
I muſt not take God's name in vain.
I muſt not work, I muſt not play,
Upon God's holy ſabbath day.
And if my parents ſpeak the word,

I muſt obey them in the Lord.
Nor ſteal, nor lie, nor ſpend my days,
In idle tales and fooliſh plays,
I muſt obey my Lord's commands,
Do ſomething with my little hands :
Remember my creator now,
In youth while time will it allow.
Young SAMUEL that little child,
He ſerv'd the Lord, liv'd undefil'd;
Him in his ſervice God employ'd,
While ELI's wicked children dy'd :
When wicked children mocking ſaid,
To a good man, *Go up bald head,*
God was diſpleas'd with them and ſent
Two bears which them in pieces rent,
I muſt not like theſe children vile,
Diſpleaſe my God, myſelf defile.
Like young ABIJAH, I muſt ſee,
That good things may be found in me,
Young King JOSIAH, that bleſſed youth,
He ſought the Lord and lov'd the truth ;
He like a King did act his part,
And follow'd God with all his heart.
The little children they did ſing,
Hoſannahs to their heavenly King.
That bleſſed child young TIMOTHY,
Did learn God's word moſt heedfully.

2

It feem'd to be his recreation,
Which made him wife unto falvation:
By faith in Chrift which he had gain'd
With prayers and tears that faith unfeign'd
Thefe good examples were for me;
Like thefe good children I must be.
Give me true faith in Chrift my Lord,
Obedience to his holy word,
No word is in the world like thine,
There's none fo pure, fweet and divine.
From thence let me thy will behold,
And love thy word above fine gold.
Make my heart in thy ftatutes found,
And make my faith and love abound.
Lord circumcife my heart to love thee:
And nothing in this world above thee:
Let me behold thy pleafed face,
And make my foul to grow in grace,
And in the knowledge of my Lord
And Saviour Chrift, and of his word.

Another.

AWAKE, arife, behold thou haft,
   Thy life a leaf, thy breath a blaft;
At night lay down prepar'd to have
Thy fleep, thy death, thy bed, thy grave.

LORD if thou lengthen out my days,
   Then let my heart fo fixed be,

That I may lengthen out thy praise,
And never turn afide from thee.

So in my end I fhall rejoice,
In thy falvation joyful be ;
My foul fhall say with loud glad voice,
JEHOVAH who is like to thee ?

Who takeft the lambs into thy arms,
And gently leadeft thofe with young,
Who faveft children from all harms,
Lord, I will praife thee with my fong.

And when my days on earth fhall end,
And I go hence and be here no more,
Give me eternity to fpend,
My G O D to praife forever more.

Another.

Good children muft,

Fear God all day,	Love Chrift alway,
Parents obey,	In fecret pray,
No falfe thing fay,	Mind little play,
By no fin ftray,	Make no delay,

In doing good.

Another.

I In the burying place may fee,
  Graves fhorter there than I,
From death's arreft no age is free,
  Young children too muft die.
My God may fuch an awful fight,

Awakening be to me!
Oh! that by early grace I might
  For death prepared be.
          Another.

NOW I lay me down to take my sleep,
  I pray the Lord my soul to keep,
If I should die before I wake,
I pray the Lord my soul to take.
          Another.

First in the morning when thou dost awake,
  To God for his grace thy petition make,
Some heavenly petition use daily to say,
That the God of heaven may bless thee alway.
    Duty to God and our neighbour.

LOVE God with all your soul & strength,
  With all your heart and mind;
And love your neighbour as yourself,
  Be faithful, just and kind.
Deal with another as you'd have
  Another deal with you:
What you're unwilling to receive,
  Be sure you never do.
    Our Saviour's Golden Rule.

BE you to others kind and true,
  As you'd have others be to you:
And neither do nor say to men,
  Whate'er you would not take again.

The Sum of the ten Commandments.

WITH all thy soul love God above,
    And as thyself thy neighbour love.

Advice to Youth. Eccle. xii.

NOW in the heat of youthful blood,
    Remember your Creator God;
Behold the months come haſt'ning on,
When you ſhall ſay, *My joys are gone.*

Behold the aged ſinner goes
Laden with guilt and heavy woes,
Down to the regions of the dead,
With endleſs curſes on his head.

The duſt returns to duſt again,
The ſoul in agonies of pain,
Aſcends to God not there to dwell,
But hears her doom and ſinks to hell.

Eternal King I fear thy name,
Teach me to know how frail I am,
And when my ſoul muſt hence remove,
Give me a manſion in thy love.

Remember thy Creator in the days of thy youth.

CHILDREN your great Creator fear,
    To him your homage pay,
While vain employments fire your blood,
    And lead your thoughts aſtray.

The due remembrance of his name
    Your first regard requires :

Till your breaſt glows with ſacred love,
  Indulge no meaner ſires.
Secure his favour, and be wiſe,
  Before theſe cheerleſs days,
When age comes on, when mirth's no more,
  And health and ſtrength decays.

Some proper Names of M E N *and* W O M E N,
  to teach Children to ſpell their own.

Men's Names.

ADam, Abel, Abraham,	Elias, Elizur,
Amos, Aaron,	Frederick, Francis,
Abijah, Andrew,	Gilbert, Giles,
Alexander, Anthony,	George, Gamalial,
Bartholomew,	Gideon, Gerſhom,
Benjamin, Barnabas,	Heman, Henry,
Benoni, Barzillai,	Hezekiah, Hugh,
Caleb, Cæſar,	John, Jonas, Iſaac,
Charles, Christopher,	Jacob, Jared, Job,
Clement, Cornelius,	James, Jonathan,
David, Daniel,	Iſrael, Joſeph,
Ephraim, Edward,	Jeremiah, Joſhua,
Edmund, Ebenezer,	Joſiah, Jedediah,
Elijah, Eliphalet,	Jabez, Joel, Judah,
Eliſha, Eleazer,	Lazarus, Luke,
Elihu, Ezekiel,	Mathew, Michael,
	Moſes, Malachi,
	Nathaniel, Nathan,

Nicholas, Noadiah, Nehemiah, Noah, Obadiah, Ozias, Paul, Peter, Philip, Phineas, Peletiah, Ralph, Richard, Samuel, Sampson, Stephen, Solomon, Seth, Simeon, Saul, Shem, Shubal, Timothy, Thomas, Titus, Theophilus, Uriah, Uzzah, Walter, William, Xerxes, Xenophon, Zachariah, Zebdiel, Zedekiah, Zadock, Zebulon, Zebediah,

Women's Names.

Abigail, Anne, Alice, Anna, Bethiah, Bridget, Cloe, Charity, Deborah, Dorothy, Dorcas, Dinah, Damaris, Elizabeth, Esther, Eunice, Eleanor, Frances, Flora, Grace, Gillet, Hannah, Huldah, Hepzibah, Henrietta, Hagar. Joanna, Jane, Jamima, Isabel, Judith, Jennet, Katharine, Katura, Kezia, Lydia, Lucretia, Lucy, Louis, Lettice, Mary, Margaret, Martha, Mehitable, Marcy, Merial, Patience, Phylis, Phebe, Priscilla, Rachel, Rebecca, Ruth, Rhode, Rose. Sarah, Susanna, Tabitha, Tamesin, Ursula, Zipporah, Zibiah

Mr. John Rogers, minister of the gospel in *London*, was the first martyr in Queen Mary's reign, and was burnt at *Smithfield, February* 14, 1554.—His wife with nine small children, and one at her breast following him to the stake; with which sorrowful sight he was not in the least daunted, but with wonderful patience died courageously for the gospel of Jesus Christ.

*Some few days before his death, he wrote the
  following Advice to his Children.*

GIVE ear my children to my words
  Whom God hath dearly bought,
Lay up his laws within your heart,
  and print them in your thoughts.
I leave you here a little book
  for you to look upon,
That you may see your father's face
  when he is dead and gone :
Who for the hope of heavenly things,
  While he did here remain,
Gave over all his golden years
  to prison and to pain.
Where I, among my iron bands,
  inclosed in the dark,
Not many days before my death,
  I did compose this work :
And for example to your youth,
  to whom I wish all good,
I send you here God's perfect truth,
  and seal it with my blood.
To you my heirs of earthly things :
  which I do leave behind,
That you may read and understand
  and keep it in your mind.
That as you have been heirs of that

that once shall wear away,
You also may possess that part,
   which never shall decay.
Keep always God before your eyes,
   with all your whole intent,
Commit no sin in any wise,
   keep his commandment.
Abhor that arrant whore of R o m e,
   and all her blasphemies,
And drink not of her cursed cup,
   obey not her decrees.
Give honor to your mother dear,
   remember well her pain,
And recompence her in her age,
   with the like love again.
Be always ready for her help,
   and let her not decay,
Remember well your father all,
   who would have been your stay.
Give of your portion to the poor,
   as riches do arise,
And from the needy naked soul,
   turn not away your eyes:
For he that doth not hear the cry
   of those that stand in need,
Shall cry himself and not be heard,
   when he does hope to speed.

If GOD hath given you increaſe,
    and bleſſed well your ſtore,
Remember you are put in truſt,
    and ſhould relieve the poor.
Beware of ſoul and filthy luſt,
    let ſuch things have no place,
Keep clean your veſſels in the **LORD**,
    that he may you embrace.
Ye are the temples of the **LORD**,
    for you are dearly bought,
And they that do defile the ſame,
    ſhall ſurely come to nought.
Be never proud by any means,
    build not your houſe too high,
But always have before your eyes,
    that you are born to die.
Defraud not him that hired is,
    your labour to ſuſtain,
But pay him ſtill without delay,
    his wages for his pain.
And as you would that other men
    againſt you ſhould proceed,
Do you the ſame to them again,
    when they do ſtand in need.
Impart your portion to the poor,
    in money and in meat

And fend the feeble fainting foul,
   of that which you do eat.
Afk counfel always of the wife,
   give ear unto the end,
And ne'er refufe the fweet rebuke
   of him that is thy friend.
Be always thankful to the LORD,
   with prayer and with praife,
Begging of him to blefs your work,
   and to direct your ways.
Seek firft, I fay, the living GOD,
   and always him adore,
And then be fure that he will blefs,
   your bafket and your ftore.
And I befeech Almighty GOD,
   replenifh you with grace,
That I may meet you in the heavens,
   and fee you face to face.
And though the fire my body burns,
   contrary to my kind,
That I cannot enjoy your love
   according to my mind :
Yet I do hope that when the heavens
   fhall vanifh like a fcroll,
I fhall fee you in perfect fhape,
   in body and in foul.
And that I may enjoy your love,

and you enjoy the land,
I do befeech the living LORD,
  to hold you in his hand.
Though here my body be adjudg'd
  in flaming fire to fry,
My foul I truft, will ftraight afcend
  to live with GOD on high.
What though this carcafe fmart awhile
  what though this life decay,
My foul I hope will be with GOD,
  and live with him for aye.
I know I am a finner born,
  from the original,
And that I do deferve to die
  by my fore-father's fall :
But by our S A V I O U R's precious **blood**,
  which on the crofs was fpilt,
Who freely offer'd up his life,
  to fave our fouls from guilt :
I hope redemption I fhall have,
  and all who in him truft,
When I fhall fee him face to face,
  and live among the juft.
Why then fhould I fear death's grim **look**
  fince CHRIST for me did die,
For King and *Cæfar*, rich and **poor**,
  the force of death muft try.

When I am chained to the ſtake,
  and fagots girt me round,
Then pray the LORD my ſoul in heaven
  may be with glory crown'd.
Come welcome death the end of fears,
  I am prepar'd to die :
Thoſe earthly flames will fend my ſoul
  up to the Lord on high.
Farewell my children to the world,
  where you muſt yet remain ;
The LORD of hoſts be your defence,
  'till we do meet again.
Farewell my true and loving wife,
  my children and my friends,
I hope in heaven to fee you all,
  when all things have their end.
If you go on to ſerve the LORD,
  as you have now begun,
You ſhall walk fafely all your days,
  until your life be done.
GOD grant you fo to end your days,
  as he ſhall think it beſt,
That I may meet you in the heavens,
  where I do hope to reſt.

OUR days begin with trouble here,
  our life is but a ſpan,

And cruel death is always near,
    fo frail a thing is man.
Then fow the feeds of grace whilſt young,
    that when thou com'ſt to die,
Thou may'ſt ſing forth that triumph ſong,
    Death where's thy victory.

Choice Sentences.

1. P R A Y i n g will make us leave ſinning, or ſinning will make us leave praying.

2. O u r weakneſs and inabilities break not the bond of our duties.

3. W H A T we are afraid to ſpeak before men, we ſhould be afraid to think before GOD.

Learn theſe four lines by heart.

H A V E communion with few,
    Be intimate with ONE,
Deal juſtly with all,
Speak evil of none.

A G U R's Prayer.

R E M O V E far from me vanities and lies ; give me neither poverty nor riches ; feed me with food convenient for me : left I be full and deny thee, and ſay, Who is the Lord ? Or left I be poor and ſteal and take the name of my GOD in vain.

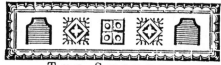

THE SHORTER
CATECHISM,

Agreed upon by the Reverend Assembly of
DIVINES at *Westminster*.

Quest. **W**HAT *is the chief end of man?*
Ans. Man's chief end is to
glorify God and enjoy him forever.

Q. 2. *What rule hath God given to direct us how we may glorify and enjoy him?*

A. The word of God which is contained
in the scriptures of the old and new testament is the only rule to direct us how we
may glorify God and enjoy him.

Q. 3. *What do the scriptures principally teach?*

A. The scriptures principally teach what
man is to believe concerning God, and what
duty God requireth of man.

Q. 4. *What is God?*

A. God is a spirit, infinite, eternal, and
unchangeable, in his being, wisdom, power,
holiness, justice, goodness and truth.

Q. 5. *Are there more Gods than one?*

A. There is but ONE only, the living and true GOD.

Q. 6. *How many persons are there in the God-head?*

A. There are three perſons in the God-head, the Father, the Son, and the Holy Ghoſt, and theſe three are one GOD, the ſame in ſubſtance, equal in power and glory.

Q. 7. *What are the decrees of God?*

A. The decrees of God are his eternal purpoſe, according to the counſel of his own will, whereby for his own glory he hath fore-ordained whatſoever comes to paſs.

Q. 8. *How doth God execute his decrees?*

A. God executeth his decrees in the works of creation and providence.

Q. 9. *What is the work of creation?*

A. The work of creation is God's making all things of nothing by the word of his pow-er, in the ſpace of ſix days, and all very good.

Q. 10. *How did God create man?*

A. God created man male & female after his own image, in knowledge, righteouſneſs and holineſs, with dominion over the creatures

Q. 11. *What are God's works of providence?*

A. God's works of providence are his moſt holy, wiſe and powerful, preſerving & governing all his creatures and all their actions.

Q. 12. *What special act of providence did God exercise towards man in the estate wherein he was created?*

A. When God had created man, he entered into a covenant of life with him upon condition of perfect obedience, forbidding him to eat of the tree of knowledge of good and evil, upon pain of death.

Q. 13. *Did our first parents continue in the estate wherein they were created?*

A. Our first parents being left to the freedom of their own will, fell from the estate wherein they were created, by sinning against God.

Q. 14. *What is sin?*

A. Sin is any want of conformity unto, or transgression of the law of God.

Q. 15. *What was the sin whereby our first parents fell from the estate wherein they were created?*

A. The sin whereby our first parents fell from the estate wherein they were created, was their eating the forbidden fruit.

Q. 16, *Did all mankind fall in* Adam's *first transgression?*

A. The covenant being made with *Adam*, not only for himself, but for his posterity.

all mankind descending from him by ordinary generation, sinned in him, and fell with him in his first transgression.

Q. 17. *Into what estate did the fall bring mankind?*

A. The fall brought mankind into an estate of sin and misery.

Q. 18. *Wherein consists the sinfulness of that estate whereinto man fell?*

A. The sinfulness of that estate whereinto man fell, consists in the guilt of *Adam's* first sin, the want of original righteousness, & the corruption of his whole nature, which is commonly called original sin, together with all actual transgressions which proceed from it.

Q. 19. *What is the misery of that estate whereinto man fell?*

A. All mankind by the fall lost communion with God, are under his wrath & curse, and so made liable to the miseries in this life, to death itself, & to the pains of hell forever.

Q. 20. *Did God leave all mankind to perish in the state of sin and misery?*

A. God having out of his mere good pleasure from all eternity elected some to everlasting life, did enter into a covenant of grace, to deliver them out of a state of fin and mifery, and to bring them into a ftate of falvation by a Redeemer.

Q. 21. *Who is the Redeemer of God's elect?*

A. The only Redeemer of God's elect, is the Lord Jefus Chrift, who being the eternal Son of God, became man, and fo was, and continues to be God and man, in two diftinct natures, and one perfon forever.

Q. 22. *How did Chrift being the Son of God become man?*

A. Chrift the Son of God became man by taking to himfelf a true body and a refonable foul, being conceived by the power of the Holy Ghoft, in the womb of the virgin *Mary*, and born of her, and yet without fin.

Q. 23. *What offices doth Chrift execute as our Redeemer?*

A. Chrift as our Redeemer executes the office of a prophet, of a prieft, & of a king, both in his eftate of humiliation and exaltation.

Q. 24. *How doth Chrift execute the office of a prophet?*

A. Chrift executeth the office of a prophet in revealing to us by his word and fpirit, the will of God for our falvation.

Q. 25. *How doth Chrift execute the office of a prieft?*

A. Chrift executeth the office of a prieft in his once offering up himfelf a facrifice to fatisfy divine juftice, and reconcile us to God, and in making continual interceffion for us.

Q. 26. *How doth Chrift execute the office of a king ?*

A. Chrift executeth the office of a king in fubduing us to himfelf, in ruling and defending us, and in reftraining and conquering all his and our enemies.

Q 27 *Wherein did Chrift's humiliation confift?*

A. Chrift's humiliation confifted in his being born and that in a low condition, made under the law, undergoing the miferies of this life, the wrath of God, and the curfed death of the crofs, in being buried and continuing under the power of death for a time.

Q. 28. *Wherein confifts Chrift's exaltation?*

A. Chrift's exaltation confifteth in his rifing again from the dead on the third day, in afcending up into heaven, and fitting at the right hand of God the Father, and in coming to judge the world at the laft day.

Q. 29. *How are we made partakers of the redemption purchased by Chrift ?*

A. We are made partakers of the redemption purchafed by Chrift by the effectual application of it to us by his holy Spirit.

Q. 30. *How doth the Spirit apply to us the redemption purchaſed by Chriſt?*

A. The Spirit applieth to us the redemption purchaſed by Chriſt, by working faith in us, and thereby uniting us to Chriſt in our effectual calling.

Q. 31. *What is effectual calling?*

A. Effectual calling is the work of God's Spirit, whereby convincing us of our ſin and miſery, enlightening our minds in the knowledge of Chriſt, and renewing our wills, he doth perſuade and enable us to embrace Jeſus Chriſt, freely offered to us in the goſpel.

Q. 32. *What benefits do they that are effectually called partake of in this life?*

A. They that are effectually called do in this life partake of juſtification, adoption, and ſanctification, and the ſeveral benefits which in this life do either accompany or flow from them.

Q. 33. *What is juſtification?*

A. Juſtification is an act of God's free grace, wherein he pardoneth all our ſins, and accepteth us as righteous in his ſight only for the righteouſneſs of Chriſt imputed to us, and received by faith alone.

Q. 34. *What is adoption?*

A. Adoption is an act of God's free grace, whereby we are received into the number, and have a right to all the privileges of the fons of God.

Q. 35. *What is fanctification?*

A. Sanctification is the work of God's free grace, whereby we are renewed in the whole man, after the image of God, and are enabled more and more to die unto fin, and live unto righteoufnefs.

Q. 36. *What are the benefits which in this life do accompany or flow from juftification, adoption and fanctification?*

A. The benefits which in this life do accompany or flow from juftification, adoption and fanctification, are affurance of God's love, peace of confcience, joy in the holy Ghoft, increase of grace, and perfeverance therein to the end.

Q. 37. *What benefits do believers receive from Chrift at their death?*

A. The fouls of believers are at their death made perfect in holinefs, and do immediately pafs into glory, and their bodies being ftill united to Chrift do reft in their graves 'till the refurrection.

Q. 38. *What benefits do believers receive from Christ at the resurrection?*

A. At the resurrection believers being raised up to glory, shall be openly acknowledged and acquitted in the day of judgment, and made perfectly blessed in the full enjoyment of God to all eternity.

Q. 39. *What is the duty which God requires of man?*

A. The duty which God requires of man, is obedience to his revealed will.

Q. 40. *What did God at first reveal to man for the rule of his obedience?*

A. The rule which God at first revealed to man for his obedience was the moral law.

Q. 41. *Where is the moral law summarily comprehended?*

A. The moral law is summarily comprehended in the ten commandments.

Q. 42. *What is the sum of the ten commandments?*

A. The sum of the ten commandments is, to love the Lord our God with all our heart, with all our soul, with all our strength, and with all our mind, and our neighbour as ourselves.

Q. 43. *What is the preface to the ten*

commandments?

A. The preface to the ten commandments is in thefe words, *I am the Lord thy God which have brought thee out of the land of* Egypt, *and out of the houfe of bondage.*

Q. 44. *What doth the preface to the ten commandments teach us?*

A. The preface to the ten commandments teacheth us, that becaufe God is the Lord, and our God and Redeemer, therefore we are bound to keep all his commandments.

Q. 45. *Which is the first commandment?*

A. The firft commandment is, *Thou fhalt have no other Gods before me.*

Q. 46. *What is required in the firft commandment?*

A. The firft commandment requireth us to know and acknowledge God, to be the only true God, and our God, and to worfhip and glorify him accordingly.

Q. 47. *What is forbidden in the first commandment?*

A. The firft commandment forbiddeth the denying or not worfhipping and glorifying the true God, as God, and our God, and the giving that worfhip and glory to any other which is due to him alone.

3

Q. 48. *What are we especially taught by these words* (before me) *in the first commandment ?*

A. These words (*before me*) in the first commandment, teach us, that God who seeth all things, taketh notice of and is much displeased with the sin of having any other God.

Q. 49. *Which is the second commandment ?*

A. The second commandment is, *Thou shalt not make unto thee any graven image, or the likeness of any thing that is in heaven above, or that is in the earth beneath, or that is in the water under the earth ; thou shalt not bow down thyself to them nor serve them, for I the Lord thy God am a jealous God, visiting the iniquities of the fathers upon the children, unto the third and fourth generation of them that hate me and shewing mercy unto thousands of them that love me & keep my commandments.*

Q. 50. *What is required in the second commandment ?*

A. The second commandment requireth the receiving, observing, & keeping pure and entire all such religious worship and ordinances, as God hath appointed in his word.

Q. 51. *What is forbidden in the second commandment ?*

A. The second commandment forbiddeth the worshipping of God by images or any other way not appointed in his word.

Q. 52. *What are the reasons annexed to the second commandment?*

A. The reasons annexed to the second commandment, are God's sovereignty over us, his propriety in us, and the zeal he hath to his own worship.

Q. 53. *Which is the third commandment?*

A. The third commandment is, *Thou shalt not take the name of the Lord thy God in vain, for the Lord will not hold him guiltless, that taketh his name in vain.*

Q. 54. *What is required in the third commandment?*

A. The third commandment requireth the holy and reverent use of God's names, titles, attributes, ordinances, word and works.

Q. 55. *What is forbidden in the third commandment?*

A. The third commandment forbiddeth all profaning or abusing of any thing whereby God maketh himself known.

Q. 56. *What is the reason annexed to the third commandment?*

A. The reason annexed to the third commandment is, That however the breakers of this commandment may escape punishment from men, yet the Lord our God will not suffer them to escape his righteous judgment.

Q. 57. *Which is the fourth commandment?*

A. The fourth commandment is, *Remember the sabbath day to keep it holy, six days shalt thou labor and do all thy work, but the seventh day is the sabbath of the Lord thy God, in it thou shalt not do any work, thou nor thy son, nor thy daughter, thy man-servant, nor thy maid servant, nor thy cattle, nor the stranger that is within thy gates, for in six days the Lord made heaven and earth, the sea and all that in them is, and rested the seventh day, wherefore the Lord blessed the sabbath day and hallowed it.*

Q. 58. *What is required in the fourth commandment?*

A. The fourth commandment requireth, the keeping holy to God such set times as he hath appointed in his word, expressly one whole day in seven to be an holy Sabbath to himself.

Q. 59. *Which day of the seven hath God appointed to be the weekly sabbath?*

A. From the beginning of the world, to the refurrection of Chrift, God appointed the feventh day of the week to be the weekly fabbath, and the firft day of the week ever fince to continue to the end of the world, which is the Chriftian Sabbath.

Q. 60. *How is the fabbath to be fanctified?*

A. The fabbath is to be fanctified by an holy refting all that day, even from fuch worldly employments and recreations as are lawful on other days, and fpending the whole time in public and private exercifes of God's worfhip, except fo much as is to be taken up in the works of neceffity and mercy.

Q. 61. *What is forbidden in the fourth commandment?*

A. The fourth commandment forbiddeth, the omiffion or carelefs performance of the duties required, and the profaning the day by idlenefs, or doing that which is in itfelf finful, or by unneceffary thoughts, words or works, about worldly employments or recreations.

Q. 62. *What are the reafons annexed to the fourth commandment?*

A. The reafons annexed to the fourth commandment, are God's allowing us fix days of the week for our own employment, his challenging a special propriety in the seventh, his own example, & his blessing the sabbath day.

Q. 63. *Which is the fifth commandment?*

A. The fifth commandment is, *Honor thy father and thy mother, that thy days may be long upon the land which the Lord thy God giveth thee.*

Q. 64. *What is required in the fifth commandment?*

A. The fifth commandment requireth the preserving the honor, and performing the duties belonging to every one in their several places and relations, as superiors, inferiors, or equals.

Q. 65. *What is forbidden in the fifth commandment?*

A. The fifth commandment forbiddeth the neglecting of, or doing any thing against the honour and duty which belongeth to every one in their several places and relations.

Q. 66. *What is the reason annexed to the fifth commandment?*

A. The reason annexed to the fifth commandment is a promise of long life and prosperity, (as far as it shall serve for God's glory and their own good) to all such as keep this commandment.

Q. 67. *Which is the sixth commandment?*

A. The fixth commandment is, *Thou fhalt not kill.*

Q. 68. *What is required in the fixth commandment?*

A. The fixth commandment requireth all lawful endeavors to preferve our own life, and the life of others.

Q. 69. *What is forbidden in the fixth commandment?*

A. The fixth commandment forbiddeth the taking away of our own life, or the life of our neighbour unjuftly, and whatfoever tendeth thereunto.

Q. 70. *Which is the feventh commandment?*

A. The feventh commandment is, *Thou fhalt not commit adultery.*

Q. 71. *What is required in the feventh commandment?*

A. The feventh commandment requireth the prefervation of our own and our neighbor's chastity, in heart, speech & behaviour.

Q. 72. *What is forbidden in the feventh commandment?*

A. The feventh commandment forbiddeth all unchafte thoughts, words and actions.

Q. 73. *Which is the eighth commandment?*

A. The eighth commandment is, *Thou*

ſhalt not ſteal.

Q. 74. *What is required in the eighth commandment ?*

A. The eighth commandment requireth the lawful procuring & furthering the wealth and outward eſtate of ourſelves and others.

Q. 75. *What is forbidden in the eighth commandment ?*

A. The eighth commandment forbiddeth whatſoever doth, or may unjuſtly hinder our own or our neighbour's wealth or outward eſtate.

Q. 76. *Which is the ninth commandment ?*

A. The ninth commandment is, *Thou ſhalt not bear falſe witneſs againſt thy neighbour.*

Q. 77. *What is required in the ninth commandment ?*

A. The ninth commandment requireth the maintaining and promoting of truth between man & man, & of our own & our neighbor's good name, eſpecially in witneſs bearing.

Q 78. *What is forbidden in the ninth commandment ?*

A. The ninth commandment forbiddeth whatſoever is prejudicial to truth, or injurious to our own or our neighbor's good name.

Q. 79. *Which is the tenth commandment ?*

A. The tenth commandment is, *Thou shalt not covet thy neighbour's house, thou shalt not covet thy neighbour's wife, nor his man-servant, nor his maid-servant, nor his ox, nor his ass, nor any thing that is thy neighbour's.*

Q. 80. *What is required in the tenth commandment?*

A. The tenth commandment requireth full contentment with our own condition, with a right and charitable frame of spirit towards our neighbour, and all that is his.

Q. 81. *What is forbidden in the tenth commandment?*

A. The tenth commandment forbiddeth all discontentment with our own estate, envying or grieving at the good of our neighbour, and all inordinate motions and affections to any thing that is his.

Q. 82. *Is any man able perfectly to keep the commandments of God?*

A. No mere man since the fall is able in this life perfectly to keep the commandments of God, but daily doth break them in thought, word and deed.

Q. 83. *Are all transgressions of the law equally heinous?*

A. Some sins in themselves, and by rea-

3*

ſon of ſeveral aggravations, are more heinous in the ſight of God than others.

Q. 84. *What doth every ſin deſerve?*

A. Every ſin deſerves God's wrath & curſe
both in this life, and that which is to come.

Q. 85. *What doth God require of us that we
may eſcape his wrath and curſe due to us for ſin?*

A. To eſcape the wrath and curſe of God
due to us for ſin, God requireth of us faith in
Jeſus Chriſt, repentance unto life, with the di-
ligent uſe of all outward means whereby Chriſt
communicateth to us the benefits of redemption. Q. 86. *What is faith in Jeſus Chriſt?*

A. Faith in Jeſus Chriſt is a ſaving grace
whereby we receive & reſt upon him alone for
ſalvation as he is offered to us in the goſpel.

Q. 87. *What is repentance unto life?*

A. Repentance unto life is a ſaving grace,
whereby a ſinner out of the true ſenſe of his
ſin and apprehenſion of the mercy of God in
Chriſt, doth with grief and hatred of his ſin
turn from it unto God, with full purpoſe of
and endeavours after new obedience.

Q. 88. *What are the outward and ordinary means whereby Chriſt communicateth to
us the benefits of redemption?*

A. The outward and ordinary means where

by Chriſt communicateth to us the benefits of redemption, are his ordinances, eſpecially the word, ſacraments and prayer ; all which are made effectual to the elect for ſalvation.

Q. 89. *How is the word made effectual to ſalvation?*

A. The ſpirit of God maketh the reading, but eſpecially the preaching of the word an effectual means of convincing and converting ſinners, and of building them up in holineſs and comfort, through faith unto ſalvation.

Q. 90. *How is the word to be read and heard that it may become effectual to ſalvation?*

A. That the word may become effectual to ſalvation, we must attend thereunto with diligence, preparation and prayer, receive it with faith and love, lay it up in our hearts, and practice it in our lives.

Q. 91 *How do the ſacraments become effectual means of ſalvation?*

A. The ſacraments become effectual means of ſalvation not from any virtue in them or in him that doth adminiſter them, but only by the bleſſing of Chriſt, and the working of the Spirit in them that by faith receive them.

Q. 92. *What is a ſacrament?*

A. A ſacrament is an holy ordinance in-

ſtituted by Chriſt, wherein by ſenſible ſigns,
Chriſt & the benefits of the new covenant are
repreſented ſealed and applied to believers.

Q. 93. *What are the ſacraments of the
New Teſtament?*

A. The ſacraments of the New Teſtament are baptiſm and the Lord's ſupper.

Q. 94. *What is baptism?*

A. Baptiſm is a ſacrament wherein the waſh-
ing of water in the name of the Father and
of the Son and of the Holy Ghoſt, doth ſignify
and ſeal our ingrafting into Chriſt and par-
taking of the benefits of the covenant of
grace, & our engagements to be the Lord's.

Q. 95. *To whom is baptism to be administered?*

A. Baptiſm is not to be adminiſtered to any
that are out of the viſible church, till they
profeſs their faith in Chriſt, and obedience
to him, but the infants of ſuch as are mem-
bers of the viſible church are to be baptized.

Q. 96. *What is the Lord's ſupper?*

A. The Lord's ſupper is a ſacrament,
wherein by giving and receiving bread and
wine according to Chriſt's appointment, his
death is ſhewed forth, and the worthy recei-
vers are not after a corporal and carnal man-
ner, but by faith made partakers of his body

and blood, with all his benefits, to their fpiritual nourifhment and growth in grace.

Q. 97. *What is required in the worthy receiving the Lord's fupper?*

A. It is required of them that would worthily partake of the Lord's fupper, that they examine themfelves of their knowledge to difcern the Lord's body, of their faith to feed upon him, of their repentance, love and new obedience, left coming unworthily, they eat and drink judgment to themfelves.

Q. 98. *What is prayer?*

A. Prayer is an offering up of our defires to God for things agreeable to his will, in the name of Chrift, with confeffion of our fins, & thankful acknowledgment of his mercies.

Q. 99. *What rule hath God given for our direction in prayer?*

A. The whole word of God is of ufe to direct us in prayer but the fpecial rule of direction is that form of prayer which Chrift taught his difciples commonly called, *The Lord's Prayer.*

Q. 100. *What doth the preface of the Lord's prayer teach us?*

A. The preface of the Lord's prayer which is *Our Father which art in heaven,* teacheth us, to draw near to God with all holy reverence and confidence, as children to a father, able and ready to help us, and that we fhould pray with and for others.

Q. 101. *What do we pray for in the firft petition?*

A. In the firft petition, which is, *Hallowed be thy name*, we pray that God would enable us and others to glorify him in all that whereby he makes himfelf known, and that he would difpofe all things to his own glory.

Q. 102. *What do we pray for in the fecond petition?*

A. In the fecond petition, which is, *Thy kingdom come*, we pray that fatan's kingdom may be deftroyed, the kingdom of grace may be advanced, ourfelves and others bro't into it, and kept in it, and that the kingdom of glory may be haftened.

Q. 103. *What do we pray for in the third petition?*

A. In the third petition, which is, *Thy will be done on earth as it is in heaven*, we pray that God by his grace would make us able and willing to know, obey and fubmit to his will in all things, as the angels do in heaven.

Q. 104. *What do we pray for in the fourth petition?*

A. In the fourth petition, which is, *Give*

us this day our daily bread, we pray, that of God's free gift we may receive a competent portion of the good things of this life, and enjoy his blessing with them.

Q. 105. *What do we pray for in the fifth petition?*

A. In the fifth petition, which is, *And forgive us our debts as we forgive our debtors*, we pray that God for Christ's sake, would freely pardon all our sins, which we are the rather encouraged to ask, because by his grace we are enabled from the heart to forgive others.

Q. 106. *What do we pray for in the sixth petition?*

A. In the sixth petition, which is, *And lead us not into temptation, but deliver us from evil*, we pray that God would either keep us from being tempted to sin, or support and deliver us when we are tempted.

Q. 107. *What doth the conclusion of the Lord's prayer teach us?*

A. The conclusion of the Lord's prayer, which is, *For thine is the kingdom, and the power, and the glory, forever*, A M E N, teacheth us, to take our encouragement in prayer from God only, and in our prayers to praise him, ascribing kingdom, power and glory to him, and in teſtimony of our deſire and aſſurance to be heard, we ſay, AMEN.

> *Bleſſed are they that do his commandments*
> *that they may have right to the tree of*
> *life, and may enter in through the gates*
> *into the city.* Rev. xxii. 14.

❈❈❈❈❈❈❈❈❈❈❈❈❈❈❈❈❈❈

SPIRITUAL MILK

FOR

American *BABES,*

Drawn out of the Breaſts of both *Teſtaments,*

for their Souls Nouriſhment.

By JOHN COTTON.

Q. *WHAT hath God done for you?*
A. God hath made me, he keepeth me, and he can ſave me.

Q. *What is God?*
A. God is a Spirit of himſelf & for himſelf.

Q. *How many Gods be there?*
A. There is but one God in three Perſons, the Father, and the Son, and the Holy Ghoſt.

Q. *How did God make you?*
A. In my firſt parents holy and righteous.

Q. *Are you then born holy and righteous.*

A. No, my firſt father ſinned and I in him.

Q. *Are you then born a ſinner?*

A. I was conceived in ſin, & born in iniquity.

Q. *What is your birth ſin?*

A. Adam's ſin imputed to me, and a corrupt nature dwelling in me.

Q. *What is your corrupt nature?*

A. My corrupt nature is empty of grace, bent unto ſin, only unto ſin, and that continually.

Q. *What is ſin?*

A. Sin is a tranſgreſſion of the law.

Q. *How many commandments of the law be there?*   A. Ten.

Q. *What is the first commandment?*

A. Thou ſhalt have no other Gods before me.

Q. *What is the meaning of this commandment?*

A. That we ſhould worſhip the only true God, and no other beſides him.

Q. *What is the ſecond commandment?*

A. Thou ſhalt not make to thyſelf any graven image, &c.

Q. *What is the meaning of this commandment?*

A. That we ſhould worſhip the only true God, with true worſhip, ſuch as he hath ordained, not ſuch as man hath invented.

Q. *What is the third commandment?*

A. Thou fhalt not take the name of the Lord thy God in vain.

Q. What is meant by the name of God?

A. God himfelf & the good things of God, whereby he is known as a man by his name, and his attributes, worfhip, word and works.

Q. What is it not to take his name in vain?

A. To make ufe of God & the good things of God to his glory, and our own good, not vainly, not irreverently, not unprofitably.

Q. Which is the fourth commandment?

A. Remember that thou keep holy the fabbath day.

Q. What is the meaning of this commandment?

A. That we fhould reft from labor, and much more from play on the Lord's day, that we may draw nigh to God in holy duties.

Q. What is the fifth commandment?

A. Honor thy father and thy mother, that thy days may be long in the land which the Lord thy God giveth thee.

Q. What are meant by father and mother?

A. All our fuperiors whether in family, fchool, church and common wealth.

Q. What is the honor due unto them?

A. Reverence, obedience, and (when I am able) recompence.

Q. What is the sixth commandment?

A. Thou shalt do no murder.

Q.What is the meaning of this commandment?

A. That we should not shorten the life or health of ourselves or others, but preserve both

Q. What is the seventh commandment?

A. Thou shalt not commit adultery.

Q. What is the sin here forbidden?

A. To defile ourselves or others with unclean lusts.

Q. What is the duty here commanded?

A. Chastity to possess our vessels in holiness and honor.

Q. What is the eighth commandment?

A. Thou shalt not steal.

Q. What is the stealth here forbidden?

A. To take away another man's **goods** without his leave, or to spend our **own** without benefit to ourselves or others.

Q. What is the duty here commanded?

A. To get our goods honestly, to keep them safely, and spend them thriftily.

Q. What is the ninth commandment?

A. Thou shalt not bear false witness against thy neighbour.

Q. What is the sin here forbidden?

A. To lie falſely, to think or ſpeak untru-
ly of ourſelves or others.

Q. What is the duty here required?

A. Truth and faithfulneſs.

Q. What is the tenth commandment?

A. Thou ſhalt not covet, &c.

Q. What is the coveting here forbidden?

A. Luſt after the things of other men,
and want of contentment with our own.

*Q. Whether have you kept all theſe com-
mandments?*

A. No, I and all men are ſinners.

Q. What are the wages of ſin?

A. Death and damnation.

Q. How then look you to be ſaved?

A. Only by Jeſus Chriſt.

Q. Who is Jeſus Chriſt?

A. The eternal Son of God, who for our ſakes
became man, that he might redeem & ſave us.

Q. How doth Chriſt redeem and ſave us?

A. By his righteous life, and bitter death,
and glorious reſurrection to life again.

*Q. How do we come to have a part & fellow-
ſhip with Chriſt in his death & reſurrection?*

A. By the power of his word and ſpirit,
which brings us to him, and keeps us in him.

Q. What is the word?

A. The holy scriptures of the prophets and apostles, the old and new testament, the law and gospel.

Q. How doth the ministry of the law bring you toward Christ?

A. By bringing me to know my sin, and the wrath of God, against me for it.

Q. What are you hereby the nearer to Christ?

A. So I come to feel my cursed estate and need of a Saviour.

Q. How doth the ministry of the Gospel help you in this cursed estate?

A. By humbling me yet more, and then raising me out of this estate.

Q. How doth the ministry of the Gospel humble you yet more?

A. By revealing the grace of the Lord Jesus in dying to save sinners, and yet convincing me of my sin in not believing on him, and of my utter insufficiency to come to him, and so I feel myself utterly lost.

Q. How doth the ministry of the gospel raise you up out of this lost estate to come to Christ?

A. By teaching me the value and virtue of the death of Christ, and the riches of his grace to lost sinners by revealing the promise of grace to such, and by ministring the Spirit of

grace to apply Chriſt, and his promiſe of
grace unto myſelf, and to keep me in him.

Q. *How doth the Spirit of grace apply Chriſt &*
his promiſe grace unto you and keep you in him?

A. By begetting in me faith to receive him,
prayer to call upon him, repentance to mourn
after him, and new obedience to ſerve him.

Q. *What is faith ?*

A. Faith is the grace of the Spirit, whereby I deny myſelf, and believe on Chriſt for
righteouſneſs and ſalvation.

Q. *What is prayer ?*

A. It is calling upon God in the name of
Chriſt by the help of the Holy Ghoſt, according to the will of God.

Q. *What is repentance ?*

A. Repentance is a grace of the Spirit,
whereby I loath my ſins, and myſelf for them
and confeſs them before the Lord, and mourn
after Chriſt for the pardon of them, and for
grace to ſerve him in newneſs of life.

Q. *What is the newneſs of life, or new obedience?*

A. Newneſs of life is a grace of the Spirit,
whereby I forſake my former luſt & vain com-
pany, and walk before the Lord in the light
of his word, and in the communion of ſaints.

Q. *What is the communion of ſaints ?*

A. It is the fellowſhip of the church in the bleſſings of the covenant of grace, and the ſeals thereof.   Q. *What is the church?*

A. It is a congregation of ſaints joined together in the bond of the covenant, to worſhip the Lord, and to edify one another in all his holy ordinances.

Q, *What is the bond of the covenant by which the church is joined together?*

A. It is the profeſſion of that covenant which God has made with his faithful people, to be a God unto them, and to their ſeed.

Q. *What doth the Lord bind his people to in this covenant?*

A. To give up themſelves & their ſeed firſt to the Lord to be his people, & then to the elders & brethren of the church to ſet forward the worſhip of God & their mutual edification.

Q. *How do they give up themſelves and their ſeed to the Lord?*

A. By receiving thro' faith the Lord & his covenant to themſelves, & to their ſeed & accordingly walking themſelves & training up their children in the ways of the covenant.

Q. *How do they give up themſelves and their ſeed to the elders and brethren of the church?*

A. By confeſſing of their ſins, and profeſsion of their faith, and of their subjection to the gospel of Christ; and so they and their seed are received into the fellowship of the church and the seals thereof.

Q. What are the seals of the covenant now in the days of the gospel?

A. Baptism and the Lord's Supper.

Q. What is done for you in baptism?

A. In baptism the washing with water is a sign and seal of my washing in the blood and spirit of Christ, and thereby of my ingrafting into Christ, of the pardon and cleansing of my sins, of my raising up out of afflictions, and also of my resurrection from the dead at the last day.

Q. What is done for you in the Lord's supper?

A. In the Lord's supper, the receiving of the bread broken and the wine poured out is a sign and seal of my receiving the communion of the body of Christ broken for me, and of his blood shed for me, and thereby of my growth in Christ, and the pardon and healing of my sins, of the fellowship of the Spirit, of my strengthening and quickening in grace, and of my sitting together with Christ on his throne of glory at the last judgment.

Q. What was the resurrection from the

dead, which was sealed up to you in baptism?

A. When Chrift fhall come in his laft judgment, all that are in their graves fhall rife again, both the juft and unjuft.

Q. What is the judgment, which is sealed up to you in the Lord's supper?

A. At the laft day we fhall all appear before the judgment feat of Chrift, to give an account of our works, and receive our reward according to them.

Q. What is the reward that fhall then be given?

A. Tho righteous fhall go into life eternal, and the wicked fhall be caft into everlafting fire with the Devil and his angels.

A DIALOGUE *between* CHRIST, YOUTH,
and the Devil. YOUTH

THofe days which God to me doth fend,
In pleafure I'm refolv'd to fpend;
Like as the birds in th' lovely spring,
Sit chirping on the bough, and fing;
Who ftraining forth thofe warbling notes,
Do make fweet mufic in their throats,
So I refolve in this my prime,
In fports and plays to fpend my time.
Sorrow and grief I'll put away,
Such things agree not with my day:

4

From clouds my morning ſhall be free ;
And nought on earth ſhall trouble me.
I will embrace each ſweet delight,
This earth affords me day and night :
Though parents grieve and me correct,
Yet I their counsel will reject.

Devil.

The reſolution which you take,
Sweet youth it doth me merry make.
If thou my counsel wilt embrace,
And ſhun the ways of truth and grace,
And learn to lie, and curſe and swear,
And be as proud as any are ;
And with thy brothers wilt fall out,
And ſiſters with vile language flout :
Yea, fight and ſcratch, and alſo bite,
Then in thee I will take delight.
If thou wilt but be rul'd by me,
An artiſt thou ſhalt quickly be,
In all my ways which lovely are,
Ther'e ſew with thee who ſhall compare.
Thy parents always diſobey ;
Don't mind at all what they do ſay :
And alſo pout and ſullen be,
And thou ſhalt be a child for me.
When others read, be thou at play,
Think not on God, don't sigh nor pray

Nor be thou such a silly fool,
To mind thy book or go to school;
But play the truant; fear not I
Will straitway help you to a lie,
Which will excuse thee from the fame,
From being whipp'd and from all blame;
Come bow to me, uphold my crown,
And I'll thee raise to high renown.

YOUTH.

These motions I will cleave unto,
And let all other counsels go;
My heart against my parents now,
Shall harden'd be, and will not bow:
I won't submit at all to them,
But all good counsels will condemn,
And what I list that do will I,
And stubborn be continually.

CHRIST.

Wilt thou, O youth make such a choice,
And thus obey the devil's voice!
Curst sinful ways wilt thou embrace,
And hate the ways of truth and grace?
Wilt thou to me a rebel prove?
And from thy parents quite remove
Thy heart also? Then shalt thou see,
What will e'er long become of thee.
Come, think on God, who did thee make,

And at his prefence dread and quake,
Remember him now in thy youth,
And let thy foul take hold of truth:
The Devil and his ways defy,
Believe him not, he doth but lie:
His ways feem fweet, but youth beware,
He for thy foul hath laid a fnare.
His fweet will into bitter turn,
If in thofe ways thou ftill wilt run,
He will thee into pieces tear,
Like lions which moft hungry are.
Grant me thy heart, thy folly leave,
And from this lion I'll thee fave;
And thou fhalt have fweet joy from me,
Which fhall laft to eternity.

YOUTH.

My heart fhall chear me in my youth,
I'll have my frolicks in good truth,
What e'er feems lovely in mine eye,
Myfelf I cannot it deny.
In my own ways I ftill will walk,
And take delight among young folk,
Who fpend their days in joy and mirth,
Nothing like that I'm fure on earth:
Thy ways, O Chrift! are not for me,
They with my age do not agree.
If I unto thy laws fhould cleave,

No more good days then should I have.

CHRIST.

Woul'st thou live long and good days see
Refrain from all iniquity :
True good alone doth from me flow,
It can't be had in things below.
Are not my ways, O youth ! for thee,
Then thou shalt never happy be ;
Nor ever shall thy soul obtain,
True good, whilst thou dost here remain.

YOUTH.

To thee, O Christ, I'll not adhere,
What thou speak'st of does not appear
Lovely to me I cannot find,
'Tis good to set or place my mind
On ways whence many sorrows spring,
And to the flesh such crosses bring,
Don't trouble me, I must fulfil,
My fleshly mind, and have my will.

CHRIST.

Unto thyself then I'll thee leave,
That Satan may thee wholly have :
Thy heart in sin shall harden'd be,
And blinded in iniquity.
And then in wrath I'll cut thee down,
Like as the grass and flowers mown ;
And to thy woe thou shalt espy,

4*

Childhood and youth are vanity;
For all such things I'll make thee know
To judgment thou shall come also.
In hell at last thy soul shall burn,
When thou thy sinful race hast run.
Consider this, think on thy end
Lest God do thee in pieces rend.

Youth.

Amazed, Lord! I now begin,
O help me and I'll leave my sin:
I tremble, and do greatly fear,
To think upon what I do hear.
Lord! I religious now will be,
And I'll from Satan turn to thee.

Devil.

Nay, foolish youth, don't change thy mind,
Unto such thoughts be not inclin'd.
Come, cheer up thy heart, rouse up, be glad:
There is no hell; why art thou sad?
Eat, drink, be merry with thy friend,
For when thou diest, that's thy last end.

Youth.

Such thoughts as these I can't receive,
Because God's word I do believe;
None shall in this destroy my faith,
Nor do I mind what Satan saith.

Devil.

Although to thee herein I yield.
Yet e'er long I ſhall win the field.
That there's a heaven I can't deny,
Yea, and a hell of miſery:
That heaven is a lovely place
I can't deny; 'tis a clear caſe;
And eaſy 'tis for to come there,
Therefore take thou no further care,
All human laws do thou obſerve,
And from old cuſtoms never ſwerve;
Do not oppoſe what great men ſay,
And thou ſhalt never go aſtray.
Thou may'ſt be drunk, and ſwear and curſe,
And ſinners like thee ne'er the worſe;
At any time thou may'ſt repent;
'Twill ſerve when all thy days are ſpent.

CHRIST.

Take heed or elſe thou art undone;
Theſe thoughts are from the wicked One,
Narrow's the way that leads to life,
Who walk therein do meet with ſtrife.
Few ſhall be ſaved, young man know,
Moſt do unto deſtruction go.
If righteous ones ſcarce ſaved be,
What will at laſt become of thee!
Oh! don't reject my precious call,
Leſt ſuddenly in hell thou fall;

Unleſs you ſoon converted be,
God's kingdom thou ſhalt never ſee.

YOUTH.

Lord, I am now at a great ſtand :
If I ſhould yield to thy command,
My comrades will me much deride,
And never more will me abide.
Moreover, this I alſo know,
Thou can'ſt at laſt great mercy ſhow.
When I am old, and pleaſure gone,
Then what thou ſay'ſt I'll think upon.

CHRIST.

Nay, hold vain youth, thy time is ſhort,
I have thy breath, I'll end thy ſport ;
Thou ſhalt not live till thou art old,
Since thou in ſin art grown ſo bold.
I in thy youth grim death will ſend,
And all thy ſports ſhall have an end.

YOUTH.

I am too young, alas to die,
Let death ſome old grey head eſpy.
O ſpare me, and I will amend,
And with thy grace my ſoul befriend,
Or elſe I am undone alas,
For I am in a woful caſe.

CHRIST.

When I did call, you would not hear,

But didſt to me turn a deaf ear;
And now in thy calamity,
I will not mind nor hear thy cry;
Thy day is paſt, begone from me,
Thou who didſt love iniquity,
Above thy ſoul and Saviour dear;
Who on the croſs great pains did bear,
My mercy thou didſt much abuſe,
And all good counſel didſt refuſe,
Juſtice will therefore vengeance take,
And thee a ſad example make.

YOUTH.

O ſpare me, Lord, forbear thy hand,
Don't cut me off who trembling ſtand,
Begging for mercy at thy door,
O let me have but one year more.

CHRIST.

If thou ſome longer time ſhould have,
Thou wouldſt again to folly cleave:
Therefore to thee I will not give,
One day on earth longer to live.

Death.

Youth, I am come to fetch thy breath,
And carry thee to th' ſhades of death,
No pity on thee can I ſhow,
Thou haſt thy God offended ſo.
Thy ſoul and body I'll divide,

Thy body in the grave I'll hide,
And thy dear foul in hell muft lie,
With Devils to eternity.

The conclufion.

Thus end the days of woful youth,
Who won't obey nor mind the truth ;
Nor hearken to what preachers fay,
But do their parents difobey.
They in their youth go down to hell,
Under eternal wrath to dwell.
Many don't live out half their days,
For cleaving unto finful ways.

The late Reverend and Venerable Mr. N A-
T H A N I E L C L A P, *of* Newport *on* Rhode
Ifland ; *his Advice to children.*

GOOD children fhould remember daily,
God their Creator, Redeemer, and
Sanctifier ; to believe in, love and ferve him;
their parents to obey them in the L O R D;
their bible and catechifm ; their baptifm ;
the L O R D's day ; the L O R D's death and refurrection ; their own death and refurrection ; and the day of judgment, when all that
are not fit for heaven muft be fent to hell.
And they fhould pray to G O D in the name
of C H R I S T, for faving grace.